With simplic
us the vital
and its worldview makes in people's lives. In
doing, she turns upside down the caricature of
Christianity as a religion of hate, anxiety, and
oppression. Instead, she shows from the Bible
and the experience of many that Christian
faith works through love, guards the heart
with divine peace, and motivates right and
compassionate action. Highly recommended!

Joel R. Beeke
President, Puritan Reformed Theological Seminary,
Grand Rapids, Michigan

Track: Worldview is an outstanding example of
what it means to understand deeply in order
to explain simply. The church owes Sharon
James a great debt of thanks for the way she
has worked through issue after issue in order
to illustrate how Jesus is the rock and the world
is sinking sand. Speaking personally, this
resource has already been a great help, as I
struggle away trying to teach my growing kids
the faith at the breakfast table. Sharon has even
put the key words I need in bold!

Rico Tice
Author, *Christianity Explored*
Senior Minister, All Souls, London

Sharon James's perspective as an historian and her diligence as an analyst of culture make everything that she writes important. But her conviction as a Christian historian and analyst makes everything she writes invaluable. Read this book to find truth, how it has changed the world, and how it has been embodied in a man who is the hope of the world.

Ben Virgo
Director, Christian Heritage London

TRACK
CULTURE

A STUDENT'S GUIDE TO
WORLDVIEW

SHARON
JAMES
SERIES EDITED BY
JOHN PERRITT

CHRISTIAN
FOCUS

rym

Scripture taken from the *Holy Bible, New International Version*®. NIV®. Copyright ©1973, 1978, 1984, 2011 by International Bible Society. Used by permission of Zondervan. All rights reserved.

Scripture quotations marked HCSB are from the *Holman Christian Standard Bible*®. HCSB®. Copyright ©1999, 2000, 2002, 2003 by Holman Bible Publishers. Used by permission.

Scripture quotations marked NASB are from the *New American Standard Bible*®, Copyright © 1960, 1962, 1963, 1968, 1971, 1972, 1973, 1975, 1977, 1995 by The Lockman Foundation Used by Permission (www.Lockman.org).

Copyright © Sharon James 2022

paperback ISBN 978-1-5271-0843-1

ebook ISBN 978-1-5271-0919-3

10 9 8 7 6 5 4 3 2 1

First published in 2022
by
Christian Focus Publications Ltd,
Geanies House, Fearn, Ross-shire,
IV20 1TW, Great Britain
www.christianfocus.com

with

Reformed Youth Ministries,
1445 Rio Road East
Suite 201D
Charlottesville,
Virginia, 22911

Cover by MOOSE77

Printed by Bell & Bain, Glasgow

MIX
Paper from
responsible sources
FSC® C007785
www.fsc.org

CONTENTS

Series Introduction

Christianity is a religion of words, because our God is a God of words. He created through words, calls Himself the Living Word, and wrote a book (filled with words) to communicate to His children. In light of this, pastors and parents should take great efforts to train the next generation to be readers. *Track* is a series designed to do exactly that.

Written for students, the *Track* series addresses a host of topics in three primary areas: Doctrine, Culture, and the Christian Life. *Track's* booklets are theologically rich, yet accessible. They seek to engage and challenge the student without dumbing things down.

One definition of a track reads: *a way that has been formed by someone else's footsteps.* The goal of the *Track* series is to point us to that 'someone else'—Jesus Christ. The One who forged a track to guide His followers. While we cannot follow this track perfectly, by His grace and Spirit He calls us to strive to stay on the path. It is our prayer that this series of books would help guide Christ's Church until He returns.

In His service,

John Perritt
RYM's Director of Resources
Series Editor

Introduction

═══════

Douglas Murray is a journalist and author, who has travelled widely. In country after country, he has seen young adults who get to their twenties, with no particular aim beyond the next night out. *'Is this all there is?'* they ask.[1] Few have any certain purpose, or any confidence about what happens when this life ends.

Murray is not a Christian, but he notes that where the Christian worldview has crumbled, the result is loss of a sense of meaning. He observes that many so-called 'churches' have been 'hollowed out from within', as confidence in the truth of Scripture has been eroded, not least by evolutionary ideas.[2] He contrasts that with the faith and assurance, even in the

---

1   Murray, D, *The Strange Death of Europe* (Bloomsbury Continuum, 2018), p. 264.

2   Ibid., pp. 211.

face of death, shown by previous generations of Christians.[3] He admits that we all know, instinctively, that we are not 'mere animals' – or 'mere consumers'.[4]

When we speak of a 'worldview', we refer to the way in which we look at the world outside ourselves; the way we answer the 'big questions' about existence. Our 'worldview' rests on the various assumptions we hold: not least whether we believe in God.

This short book shows that the Christian worldview explains **why**, as human beings, we are certainly not just animals or consumers. The Christian worldview provides certain hope for this life and eternity, hope not only for individuals, but for the whole cosmos.

---

3   Ibid., p. 223.

4   Ibid., p. 267.

1. DIGNITY: Created in the Image of God

Twenty-six year-old Heidi Crowter loves God, loves life, loves her husband – and is a passionate campaigner. In 2021 she brought a legal challenge against the government of the United Kingdom, over a law which discriminates against unborn babies with disabilities. Heidi was born with Down's syndrome.[1] As a teenager, she was cruelly trolled on social media. 'It was hurtful', she says. 'When I hear things like that, I go to the Bible: "I praise you because I am fearfully and

---

[1] Down syndrome (or Down's syndrome) refers to a condition where a child is born with an extra copy of their 21st chromosome (about 1 in 700 babies in the US). They may have some developmental delays and disabilities, but many people with this syndrome enjoy happy and fulfilled lives. https://www.healthline.com/health/down-syndrome#causes (accessed 24 January, 2022).

wonderfully made" (Ps. 139:14). It reminds me what **God** thinks about me.'[2]

'JUST A TUMOUR ON THE EARTH'?

On The Origin of Species by Charles Darwin was published in 1859. It led to an increased acceptance of evolutionary theory. In turn, that fed into a worldview which insisted that there is no Creator God, and we are here by chance. Today, many assume that we are just material beings, shaped by chemical, physical and economic forces.

That's a 'naturalistic' worldview. It implies there's no ultimate 'purpose' for our existence at all, and that there's no reason to see human beings as possessing unique dignity. We're just on a continuum with the rest of nature.

Radical green activist, **Pentti Linkola (1932-2020)**, insisted that humans are like a tumour on the earth, consuming more than our fair share of nature's resources. Logically, he argued, the majority of humans should be

---

2   https://www.theguardian.com/society/2018/dec/03/ my-life-is-just-as-important-as-everybody-elses- meet-the-disability-leaders (accessed 13 August, 2021).

killed.[3] A growing number of radical activists regard humans as the 'enemy' of the planet. They want to give legal rights to animals and plants.[4]

Others don't go that far. But they'd argue that if we just evolved, the good of the species is the most important thing. Arguably, we should get rid of weaker people, and those who are 'useless' to others. Some believe that some human lives are 'not worth living'. Those who suffer intense pain, or terminal illness should be helped to die. Those with disabilities should be aborted before birth.

But evolution is 'a theory in crisis'![5] It is an observable fact only at a small scale: the variations which are usually called **micro-evolution.** An increasing number of scientists question the way in which Darwin 'jumped' from **micro-evolution** to **macro-evolution**.[6]

---

3   Pentti Linkola, *Human Flood*, http://www. penttilinkola.com/pentti_linkola/ecofascism_ writings/humanflood/ (accessed 28 July, 2021).

4   https://waronhumans.com/the-war-on-humans-documentary/ (accessed 24 January, 2022).

5   Denton, M, *Evolution: A Theory in Crisis* (Adler and Adler Publishers, 1986).

6   Johnson, P E, 'Evolution: Fact or Fantasy?' *Apologetics Study Bible* (Holman Bible Publishers, 2007), p. 7.

The concept of macro-evolution has been challenged by the discovery that the universe had a beginning; the discovery of 'fine tuning' in the universe;[7] and the discovery of information in every cell. Each cell is filled with exquisite machinery. One pinhead of DNA could hold enough information to fill a stack of books stretching from the earth to the moon 500 times.[8] **God has left His signature in every cell.**[9]

THE DIGNITY OF EVERY PERSON

Then God said, 'Let us make man in our image, in our likeness, and let them rule over the fish of the sea and the birds of the sky,

---

7   The various conditions on earth are precisely balanced in order to support life, in a way so precise that it cannot reasonably be explained by chance. McDermott, G R, *Everyday Glory: The Revelation of God in all of Reality* (Baker Academic, 2018), pp. 63-80.

8   'DNA the Language of Life', *Answers in Genesis*, 1 July, 2008, https://answersingenesis.org/genetics/dna-similarities/dna-a-summary/ (accessed 30 December, 2020).

9   This phrase is taken from the title of a book by Stephen C Meyer, *Signature in the Cell: DNA and the Evidence for Intelligent Design* (Harper One, 2009).

over the livestock, over all the earth, and over all the creatures that move along the ground.'

So God created man in his own image,
in the image of God he created him;
male and female he created them.

God blessed them and said to them, 'Be fruitful and increase in number; fill the earth and subdue it. Rule over the fish of the sea and the birds of the air and over every living creature that moves on the ground.' (Gen. 1:26-28)

The first chapter of the Bible is clear. *Every* human being is created by God in His image, and has dignity and worth. Each time a male sperm fertilises a female egg, a unique life begins. After conception, no new genetic information is added. The Christian worldview affirms that *every human life* should be valued from conception right through to natural death.

The sixth commandment, 'You shall not murder',[10] is placed on the conscience of every person. God is angry at all wrongful taking of human life.[11] And yet, globally, more than

---

10   Exodus 20:13.

11   Genesis 9:6.

seventy million unborn human lives are ended every year. Abortion is also horribly damaging for the mother. Tragically, many women are coerced into it.

God is also angry if we treat other people badly, or even look down on any person made in His image:

Whoever oppresses the poor shows contempt for their Maker, but whoever is kind to the needy honours God. (Prov. 14:31)

The celebrity filling up your social media? Made in the image of God. The homeless person who sits outside the supermarket each day? Made in the image of God. The greatest possible affirmation of human dignity, is the fact that God Himself became human, in the person of the Lord Jesus Christ.

THE UNITY OF THE HUMAN RACE

Evolutionary ideas gave rise to the flawed 'science' of eugenics. This fed into the evil idea of racial supremacy.

Racism is an ugly reality. **Shelby Steele (born 1946)**, an American author, remembers that as a child, whenever he drove with his dad into a new town, they had to look for places

16

to eat where they would not be turned away because of their skin colour.[12]

All forms of racism are evil, because the Bible teaches the essential **unity of the human race.** We are all descended from the same first parents.[13]

> ***From one man*** *he made all the nations, that they should inhabit the whole earth; and he marked out their appointed times in history and the boundaries of their lands. (Acts 17:26)*

We are all more closely related than most people realise.[14] There are no 'absolute' identities of 'black' or 'white'.

12 Steele, S, *White Guilt: How Blacks and Whites Together Destroyed the Promise of the Civil Rights Era* (Harper Perennial, 2006), p. 8.

13 Genesis 1:26-28; Matthew 19:4; Acts 17:26; Romans 5:12 ff; 1 Corinthians 15:21f, 45f, Bavinck, H, *Reformed Dogmatics*, Volume 2 (Baker Academic, 2004), pp. 523-26.

14 Jeanson, N, https://answersingenesis.org/genetics/shocking-and-glorious-new-science-human-race-ethnicity/ (accessed 30 December, 2020); McDermott, G R, 'Misunderstanding Race and the Bible', *Public Discourse*, 20 October, 2020, https://www.thepublicdiscourse.com/2020/10/72125/ (accessed 22 October, 2020). For discussion of Critical Race Theory, see James, S, *The Lies we are Told: The Truth We Must Hold* (Christian Focus Publications, 2022).

Some today claim that Christianity is a 'Western' religion. In fact, it's the world's first truly global religion! A third of the world's population are Christian, at least in name. Christianity is growing fastest *outside* the West. And across the world, Christians are following Christ, sacrificially serving those who are suffering from injustice and abuse.

In India, for example, where the great majority are Hindu, a large section of the population, the Dalits, are still, despite theoretical legal protection, regarded as 'untouchable'. The caste system creates an ocean of abuse and suffering. But many Indian Christians are extending practical and legal help to Dalits: medical clinics, primary schools, adult literacy classes, vocational and business training and more. Many Dalit people are equipped with the education that enables them to escape dire poverty. Some Indian Christians work tirelessly for the release of those who are held in labour slavery in harsh and dangerous conditions.[15] Most importantly, Dalits are offered spiritual hope, and a sense of dignity.[16]

---

15 https://www.ijmuk.org/ (accessed 26 January, 2022).

16 https://www.om.org/dk/en/news/freeing-dalits (accessed 26 January, 2022).

When we see examples of cruelty, oppression and wrongful discrimination, the fact that we care at all indicates that we've been made in the image of the God of justice. God cares. So should we.

That's why Heidi Crowter willingly sacrifices time, and resources, to campaign for those with Down's syndrome. She challenges people to look past her disability, to see that her life is 'just as important and just as joyful as everybody else's'. She knows that God made her, and God loves her.

Main point

Every human being is created by God in His image, and has dignity and worth.

Questions for Reflection

- How does a naturalistic worldview undermine the uniqueness of human dignity?
- Why should all human life be valued?
- Why is it wrong to claim that Christianity is a 'Western' and oppressive religion?

2. JOY: Created to Praise and Glorify God

Imagine this scenario. One of your best friends is about to have a birthday. You marked the date in your calendar. You thought long and hard about what they'd really like as a gift. Finally you chose the present, wrapped it nicely and shipped it to their house. You look forward to hearing how much they enjoyed your gift. But they never think to say 'thank you!'

Ingratitude is not pleasant! Sadly, we've probably all failed at some points to thank or appreciate others.

CREATED FOR PRAISE

The *worst* ingratitude is when we fail to give thanks to our Creator. Our life, and all we enjoy, are His free gift to us. God pours His love out to all of His creation. When our eyes are opened to see His magnificent beauty, the only possible response is praise:

*Let them **give thanks** to the Lord for His faithful love and His wonderful works for all humanity. (Ps. 107:21, HCSB)*

Today we're often told that we must 'find our own identity'. In reality, we can only really know who **we** are, when we realise **who** created us, and **why**. We're not just products of chance. We're created by God, to know and enjoy Him. That is our 'purpose' or 'end' in life.[1]

As a small child I learned four basic biblical truths:

- *Who made you?* God made me
- *What else did God make?* God made all things
- *Why did God make you and all things?* For His own glory
- *How can you glorify God?* By loving Him and doing what He commands

We were created to obey and worship God. As long as our first parents obeyed their Creator, they were *holy and happy*. As soon as they disobeyed, they plunged into a state of *sin and misery*. Because of that first sin, we also,

---

1   Westminster Shorter Catechism, Question 1.

by nature, don't want to obey or worship our Maker.[2]

THE DISASTROUS EXCHANGE

Our culture is hostile to the biblical worldview. The apostle Paul lived in a culture even more hostile than ours. But he insisted that **everyone** has enough information (in nature and in their own conscience) to know that there's a God we should praise. 'They **knew God**', he wrote, but 'they neither glorified Him as God nor gave thanks to Him'. They suppressed the truth about God (that should have led them to praise), and exchanged it for a lie:

The wrath of God is being revealed from heaven against all the godlessness and wickedness of men who ***suppress the truth*** *by their wickedness, since what may be known about God is* ***plain to them***, *because God has made it* ***plain to them***. *For since the creation of the world God's invisible qualities – his eternal power and divine nature – have been* ***clearly seen***, *being understood from what is made, so that men are without excuse.* ***For although they knew God, they neither glorified him as God nor gave thanks to***

2   Romans 3:23; 5:12.

him, *but their thinking became futile and their foolish hearts were darkened. Although they claimed to be wise, they became fools and exchanged the glory of the immortal God for images made to look like a mortal human being and birds and animals and reptiles. Therefore God gave them over in the sinful desires of their hearts to sexual impurity for the degrading of their bodies with one another.* ***They exchanged the truth about God for a lie,*** *and worshipped and served created things rather than the Creator—who is forever praised. Amen. (Rom. 1:18-25)*

As human beings we are created to worship. When we refuse to worship our Creator, we worship created things instead. We don't thank God for our lives, and for all that we enjoy. We prioritise ourselves.

But living for self, and failing to praise and obey our Creator, is a sin against God. And it cuts us off from our original purpose as human beings, which is to know and love the One who made us.

ETERNAL JOY

By God's grace, we **can** be liberated to fulfil our original purpose. When we're brought into relationship with God, through the saving work of Christ, we can praise Him both for our creation and our salvation. Praising, loving, and knowing our Creator and Saviour is more wonderful than anything else. It's worth living for. It's worth dying for.

This may be surprising to some, but more people were killed for their faith in Christ in the twentieth century than in all previous centuries combined. Many of them were young people. In the Soviet Union, for example, Christianity was absolutely forbidden. But in countless schools, Christian children would openly testify of Christ, and even insist on singing hymns. They were often beaten and sent off to atheist boarding schools where they were horribly treated.

Twelve-year-old Valya was forced to become a member of the communist young pioneers. But even as her teacher read out the communist oath, Valya burst out into song: '*We will stand firm for Christ*'.[3]

Varia was one of the teens who often tormented Christian pupils. When she was eighteen, she was converted through the loving

---

3   dc Talk, *Jesus Freaks: Stories of those who Stood for Jesus* (Eagle Publishing, 2000), pp. 278-9.

witness of a friend. At a school assembly, after the Communist anthem had been sung, she boldly walked up to the front and sang a hymn beginning with the words: '*I am not ashamed to proclaim Christ*'. She was sent to a labour camp.[4]

Young believers continued to sing praises, even in the labour camps. Their joy in God could not be suppressed. Many were killed. For them, death was promotion! It was their entry to unbroken enjoyment of God.

Today, young people are often told that life is about finding whatever makes them happy. 'You do you!' they are told. They are not offered any ultimate meaning or purpose. Unsurprisingly, but tragically, many young people are suffering depression and anxiety.

By contrast, those young believers in the Soviet Union suffered appallingly, but they had joy and assurance. They knew the ultimate purpose of life: to glorify and enjoy God for ever.

Main point

Our lives, and all we have, are gifts from God; our response must be willing and joyful praise.

4   Ibid., pp. 100-2.

Questions for Reflection

- Why are we so offended by ingratitude?
- The Bible calls us to give thanks to God – why?
- Read Psalm 100. What is the connection between thanksgiving and joy?

3. PURPOSE: Created to Represent God on this Earth

Before 1960, suicide was rare among American young people. Today it's the second leading cause of death for teens and young adults (after car accidents).[1] Recently, one young man wrote:

> *… so many people my age are suffering from anxiety, depression, and other mental health problems. Drug usage, alcohol abuse, and a hook-up culture are blankets of comfort for people who have no meaning or purpose in life anymore … many of us feel hopeless and aimless in life. We are living in a society that promotes people to do whatever makes them happy, even if the consequences are dire ….[2]*

1   https://www.pbs.org/newshour/nation/suicide-among-teens-and-young-adults-reaches-highest-level-since-2000 (accessed 29 July, 2021).

2   Dreher, R, 'Letter from a Struggling Young Man', *The American Conservative*, (January 5, 2021)

Many have been brought up to think that life is **'all about me'.** But if the main purpose of life is to fulfil ourselves, why go on living if life does not deliver our desires?

A GRAND PURPOSE

We are not just here to fulfil our own ambitions! We have been created with a far greater purpose.

The triune God created everything in the cosmos 'very good'.[3] At the pinnacle of creation, man and woman were made in His image. We are not just here by chance. We have a grand purpose or 'end'.[4] God created us to know and love Him, and to represent Him on this earth.

God is the Great King. Our first parents were commanded to rule and manage the creation on His behalf:

> *Be fruitful and increase* in number, *fill the earth and subdue it. Rule over the fish of the sea and the birds of the air and over every*

---

https://www.theamericanconservative.com/dreher/benedict-option-letter-from-struggling-young-man-houellebecq/ (accessed 4 February, 2021).

3   Genesis 1.

4   The Greek word for this is 'telos'.

living creature that moves along the ground.
(Gen. 1:28).

Adam and Eve, and those who follow them, were to fill the earth with more human beings. God provided, and still provides, an astonishing array of natural resources to be developed. Man and woman were given capacity to develop these, by means of reason, creativity, intelligence, and hard work. They were given the dignity of being **co-creators** with God as they had children, and the dignity of being **co-workers** as they managed the earth.

Nature would reach its potential only by means of human skill, diligence and creativity.[5] The earth's resources, including the other living creatures, were to be carefully looked after. But these resources were to be used for the benefit of humankind.[6] Humans are to:

---

5   Genesis 2:15.

6   We are to care for both animals, and the natural world (Prov. 12:10; Deut. 20:19-20), but humans take priority in value (Matt. 6:26; 10:31). The earth is here for the use and benefit of human beings (Gen. 3:18; 9:3). Christians believe that God has given humans the responsibility to manage the earth on His behalf, many are also deeply concerned about issues of caring well for creation. Evangelicals in the

... explore the resources of the earth, to cultivate its land, to mine its buried treasures. They are called by God to develop all the potentialities found in nature and humankind as a whole. [They are] to develop not only agriculture, horticulture and animal husbandry, but also science, technology, and art.[7]

Good stewardship means due care of the environment, and regard for the preservation of the earth for future generations. Equally, the resources of the earth, including other living creatures, have been given to humans for our benefit and blessing. We are permitted to use other living creatures for food:

Then God said, 'Behold, I have given you every seed-bearing plant on the face of all the earth, and every tree whose fruit contains seed. They will be yours for food.' (Gen. 1:29)

Every living creature will be food for you; as I gave the green plants, I have given you everything. (Gen. 9:3, HCSB)[8]

18th and 19th centuries took the lead on introducing measures to improve animal welfare.

7   Hoekema, A A, *Created in God's Image* (Eerdmans, 1986), p. 79.

8   See also Romans 14:2-3.

God has good designs for human society. He has given us reason and conscience, and the capacity for relationship, morality and justice. The physical creation (nature) and the way we order our communities (society) should be the arena in which God is glorified. In the words of the reformer John Calvin, it's all *'a dazzling theatre'* of God's glory.[9]

Tragically, our first parents rebelled against their Creator and King. The creation commands were not revoked, but childbearing and work would both now be attended with pain and frustration.[10] As sinful people we don't rule over the world as we were intended to do. We often exploit it rather than manage it. And sin disrupts all our relationships (including family relationships).

Wonderfully, Genesis 3 points forward to the One who would ultimately come as the perfect representative of God on this earth, and the One who would reverse each aspect of the curse.[11]

---

9   Calvin, J, *The Institutes*, 1:5:8.

10   Genesis 3:16-19.

11   Genesis 3:15.

FINDING PURPOSE IN LOVING GOD AND OTHERS

Even after the entry of sin in the world, God continues to show kindness to all.[12] We still have the dignity of serving others as we play our part in work, at school, church, family and community. We're 'wired up' as human beings to find satisfaction in loving and caring. It's an essential element of being made in the image of a relational and personal God.

In a fallen world, our various experiences of suffering, injustice or tragedy can make us bitter. We can be released from that destructive resentment when we find purpose and joy in loving God and serving others.

In June 1972, a nine-year-old Vietnamese girl was caught in a napalm attack, and suffered life-changing burns all over her body. She was left with physical and psychological scars. She was also consumed with anger and hate. Years later, when Kim Phuc became a Christian, she was released *from* bitterness, and freed *to* love and serve. She devotes herself to providing

---

12 See chapter 5.

medical and psychological support to child victims of war.[13]

The most fulfilled and joyful people I have known are those who take joy in serving others. Those who focus on self-fulfilment often end up miserable and resentful.

Think back to that young man who lamented the loss of meaning and purpose among his peers. He's a Christian believer, but has been disappointed to find that the churches around him compromise with the surrounding worldview, and don't effectively reach out to disillusioned young people.[14] All too often they buy into the current idea that life is all about our own fulfilment and flourishing, without any need to obey and submit to the God who created us.

We need a new generation of Christians who confidently believe, and proclaim, that we are created to love and glorify our Creator. We represent Him on this earth as we serve Him and love our neighbour. We can continue to enjoy and glorify Him forever in the new heavens and earth.

---

13 James, S, *How Christianity Transformed the World*, pp. 101, 126.

14 Dreher, R, 'Letter from a Struggling Young Man', *The American Conservative* (January 5, 2021).

Main point

We are here to know and enjoy our Creator, and to obey Him as we serve others.

Questions for Reflection

- Why do you think a self-centred worldview fails to give purpose or satisfaction?
- Can you think of people you have known who have found joy and satisfaction in serving the needs of others?

4. SUFFERING AND INJUSTICE: What's Gone Wrong?

Marks and scars on Jyothi's body bore witness to abuse and exploitation … threatened with trafficking into servitude, she came to one of our shelters and began the healing process.[1]

Everyday we're reminded in the news of the injustice and misery endured by many. Suffering is a reality in a fallen world. To find the truth about what's gone wrong with the world, we have to go back to the beginning of the Bible.

REBELLION AGAINST GOD

God is the Creator and King. Those created by Him owe Him obedience. When God placed our first parents in the Garden of Eden, He gave one command:

---

1   Dignity Freedom Network, India; this is a true story but with name changed. https://dfn.org.uk/ (accessed 30 July, 2021).

*And the LORD God commanded him, 'You may eat freely from every tree of the garden, but **you must not eat from the tree of the knowledge of good and evil**; for in the day that you eat of it, you will surely die.' (Gen. 2:16-17)*

God gave our first parents moral freedom. Would they choose obedience to their Creator? Or would they defy His authority?

Satan, God's enemy, set out to spoil God's good design for the world. He is the father of lies,[2] and he deceived the woman. 'You will not surely die!' he assured her. She disobeyed God's command. So did her husband.[3] The perfect relationship between God and His creation, was broken.[4] Enmity within human relationships followed.[5]

Human blood was shed for the first time, when Cain killed his brother Abel.[6] Ever since, violence, injustice, death and misery have characterised every society, and every age. Sin has spoiled the social order of family,

2   John 8:44.

3   Genesis 3:6.

4   Genesis 3:10.

5   Genesis 3:12.

6   Genesis 4:8.

communities and nations. Sin has spoiled the natural order as well. Animals suffer. Seas are polluted. Ground is over-used. Forests are badly managed.

God warned Adam that if he disobeyed the command, and ate from the Tree of the Knowledge of good and evil, he would 'certainly die'.[7] Disobedience introduced death into a world that would not otherwise have known death. Adam would ultimately die, as would all his descendants.[8] But physical death is not the end for human beings, we are immortal souls. Our bodies will be raised, and we will live forever, either in the presence of God, or banished from Him. Eternal banishment from God is described in the Bible as 'the second death',[9] but that does not mean the end of existence. It means hell: the just punishment that we all deserve for our rejection of our good Creator.[10]

---

7   Genesis 2:17.

8   1 Corinthians 15:22.

9   Revelation 20:14-15.

10   Matthew 5:22; 10:28; Luke 12:5.

THE GOD OF JUSTICE

We are angry when we see suffering, misery and injustice. God is infinitely more angry. Every sin is an offence, not only against the victim, but also against their Creator:

Whoever mocks the poor shows contempt for their Maker; whoever gloats over disaster will not go unpunished. (Prov. 17:5)

The very fact that we are outraged when we see injustice, witnesses to the fact that we are created in God's image. He is a God of justice, and has given us an innate sense of justice too. Consider this on a small scale. Have you ever heard children fight over the last cookie or piece of cake? Even little children object if they think their sibling has been given more sweets than they have! 'That's unfair!' they shout.

The blame for evil is not just found 'out there'. Which of us has a perfectly clear conscience? Which of us has always treated others as we would ourselves wish to be treated? Which of us has loved God with all our heart? We are part of the problem.

However hard we try to do the right thing, or attempt to love God, the instinct to please ourselves rises up. The problem is not just that we do, think, and say wrong things. We **are** rebellious by nature. Spiritually we are **all** 'dead' in sin. The Bible explains that not only are we 'one race' physically speaking, we are 'one race' morally speaking. When our first parents sinned, we sinned as well.[11] We **all** need new life.

BY WHAT STANDARD?

God has placed awareness of His moral law in the conscience of every human being.[12] The Ten Commandments reflect God's own moral character.[13] Uniquely among the rest of the laws recorded in the early books of the Bible, God didn't just *speak* of them to Moses, He wrote them down.[14] They are for all times and for all people.[15] Morality is not relative. We are all morally accountable. Our Creator will judge

---

11 Romans 5:12,18; 1 Corinthians 15:21-22; Ephesians 2:1.

12 Romans 2:15.

13 See Appendix C.

14 Exodus 31:18.

15 https://www.christian.org.uk/resource/the-moral-law (Last accessed March 2022.) https://www.christian.org.uk/resource/the-threefold-division-of-the-law (Last accessed March 2022.)

every one of us according to the law He has placed in our hearts.

It is destined for people to die once, and after this comes judgment. (Heb. 9:27, NASB)

For we must all appear before the judgment seat of Christ. (2 Cor. 5:10)

By God's standard every one of us is guilty. The moral law shows us our guilt and points to the right way to live. But by ourselves we cannot obey it perfectly. That's where God's grace comes in. He freely offers new life and new power to love Him and His law.

Only the biblical worldview fully accounts for **both** the evil in the world **and** the good in the world. **Every** individual human being is **both** infinitely valuable (made in the image of God) **and** utterly sinful (naturally in rebellion against God).

Think back to little Jyothi. The biblical worldview explains why humans are capable of such cruelty. It clarifies the reality of human sinfulness. It also explains why we are outraged when we hear of a little girl like Jyothi being abused. We have a conscience because we are made in the image of God. Indeed, some people are even willing to sacrifice their own safety in order to rescue those trapped in abuse. That's why Christians in the Dignity Freedom Network provide places of safety for victims like Jyothi.

> *Given a place in one of our schools, she was soon excelling. 'I want to be a doctor', she says, 'I want to treat patients who need help like I did'. Jyothi graduated with distinction and is now studying sciences at college prior to doctor training. From destitution to top of the class!*[16]

The gospel is good news to abused and abuser alike. We all, equally, stand in need of God's grace.

Main point

We are all sinners, in need of God's grace.

Questions for Reflection

• How would you respond to the claim that morality is 'relative' (i.e. We can choose our own rules)?

---

16 https://dfn.org.uk/ (accessed 30 July, 2021).

- If we evolved as a result of random chance, how could we explain the fact that we all have a conscience?
- What would you say to the claim that the Ten Commandments are only relevant to Christians?

5. GOD'S KINDNESS TO ALL: Evil Restrained

Human sinfulness means that we see injustice, greed, exploitation, war and pollution.

Creation itself was affected by sin, which is why we see disease and natural disasters.

But the world is not as violent, chaotic and ugly as it could be. After the universal flood, God promised Noah:

As long as the earth endures, seed-time and harvest, cold and heat, summer and winter, day and night will never cease. (Gen. 8:22)

We see order in creation. The Lord Jesus Christ sustains the whole universe by His power.[1] God cares for, waters and enriches the earth. He designed nature to provide a continual supply of food as seeds germinate and ripen.[2] He is 'good to all, and has compassion on all he

---

1   Hebrews 1:3; Colossians 1:17.
2   Psalm 65:9; 104:10-11,14, 27; 136:25; Acts 14:17.

has made'.[3] He is 'kind to the ungrateful and wicked'.[4]

> *He causes his sun to rise on the evil and the good, and sends rain on the righteous and the unrighteous. (Matt. 5:45)*

The kindness God extends to all (whether or not they acknowledge Him), is sometimes described as His 'common grace', or 'everyday grace', to distinguish it from His saving grace.[5]

EVIL RESTRAINED

As well as pouring out blessings to all, God restrains sin. He gives everyone a conscience.[6] All people are made in His image, and although that is marred by sin, it's not eliminated. That's why we sometimes see non-Christians acting in noble, moral and heroic ways. God has also ordained social structures to restrain sin. Civil society: families, societies, and nations, are the 'community' of common grace. Whether we are believers or not, we are part of these communities.

---

3   Psalm 145:9.

4   Luke 6:35.

5   https://www.christian.org.uk/wp-content/uploads/common-grace-leaflet.pdf (Last accessed March 2022.)

6   Romans 2:15.

After the flood, Noah was told that if anyone murdered another person, the crime is so serious that the murderer's life should be taken.[7] This was the institution of civil government and law. And, after the building of the Tower of Babel, God divided humanity into different nations.[8] This was a way of protecting sinful humanity against global government, which could form the ultimate tyranny.

The God of Justice expects rulers to rule justly. They too have a conscience and know that wrong should be punished. God watches over the different nations and is angry when rulers acquit the guilty, accuse the innocent, accept bribes, and govern in self-interest.

Acquitting the guilty and condemning the innocent—the Lord detests them both. (Prov. 17:15)

In affairs of justice rulers are to be impartial. The Bible also teaches that it is a special responsibility of government leaders to make sure the poor are treated fairly.[9]

---

7   Genesis 9:6.

8   Genesis 11:5-9.

9   Grudem, W, Asmus, B, *The Poverty of Nations: A Sustainable Solution* (Crossway, 2014), pp. 40-1.

If a king judges the poor with fairness, his throne will always be secure. (Prov. 29:14)

Rulers will have to answer to their Maker at the last day. Paul describes them as 'God's servants':

Let everyone be subject to the governing authorities, for there is no authority except that which God has established. The authorities that exist have been established by God. Consequently, whoever rebels against the authority is rebelling against what God has instituted, and those who do so will bring judgment on themselves. For rulers hold no terror for those who do right, but for those who do wrong. Do you want to be free from fear of the one in authority? Then do what is right and you will be commended. For the one in authority is God's servant for your good. But if you do wrong, be afraid, for rulers do not bear the sword for no reason. They are God's servants, agents of wrath to bring punishment on the wrongdoer. (Rom. 13:1-4)[10]

Rulers are to restrain evil, so governments should protect citizens from crime, from foreign

---

10   There's a similar passage in 1 Peter 2:13-17.

invasion, from bribery and corruption, and where possible from the spread of epidemics of disease. They should try to protect natural resources from careless human destruction.[11]

Rulers are to promote good, so governments should promote universal education, and laws that protect stable family structures. They should protect the freedoms of both women and men, and people of all races and religions. They should protect the freedoms of citizens to own property and buy and sell, to relocate and live anywhere within a nation.[12]

'GIVE TO CAESAR WHAT IS CAESAR'S AND TO GOD WHAT IS GOD'S'

During the twentieth century the idea gained ground that we are not accountable to anyone other than ourselves, and that all authority structures are repressive. It is true that in a fallen world authorities may abuse power. But abolishing them leads to disorder and anarchy. If we hear calls to *'Smash the police'*, we need to realise that a breakdown of law and order is always catastrophic for the most vulnerable in society.

---

11 Grudem, W, Asmus, B, *The Poverty of Nations*, pp. 250-1.

12 Ibid., chapters 7 and 8.

The Roman Empire was wicked and dissolute. Even in that context, Christian believers were commanded to submit to, and pray for, their rulers. A state exercising law and order is still a great benefit to citizens, compared to a state of anarchy or civil war. When there is no civil authority, disorder prevails. During the 1980s there was no functioning government in Somalia. The result was destitution and terror for the citizens of that country.

We are to pray for and submit to governments, because where there is order, people can live in security, and the gospel can be preached.[13] Many today assume that *any* submission to authority is demeaning. But our pattern of submission is the Lord Jesus Christ. He delighted to obey His Father.[14] Biblical commands to submit to authority are always to be limited by our greater allegiance to our God. When Jesus was asked about paying taxes, He replied, 'give to the Emperor the things that are the Emperor's and to God the things that are God's'.[15] The emperor (or the government), is not God!

---

13 1 Timothy 2:1-4.

14 John 4:34.

15 Luke 20:25; cf., Matthew 22:21; Mark 12:17.

Rulers are answerable to their Creator, which means that they don't have absolute power over those under them. If a state oversteps the bounds of authority, (for example by commanding citizens to disobey God's law, or forbidding Christians to preach the gospel), we should attempt to use legal means to challenge such overreach. Through history, Christians have worked for legal and social reforms.[16] But, ultimately we may need to say: 'We must obey God rather than men.'[17]

In a fallen world, we will never know universal or perfect justice. One day Christ will return as Judge. All injustice and oppression will then be judged. A new heavens and a new earth will be inaugurated. This fallen creation will be restored and recreated to what God originally intended it to be. Only then will there be total justice. Until that time, we can be thankful that God continues to bless the world, that the worst effects of sin are restrained, and that the gospel is proclaimed.

---

16 For more on this, see my book *How Christianity Transformed the World* (Christian Focus, 2021).

17 Acts 5:29.

Main point

God has ordained structures of civil authority to restrain evil.

Questions for Reflection

- What are the limitations on the power of human governments?
- Why are we commanded to pray for those in authority over us? (1 Tim. 2:1-4)
- Take time to pray for your local and national government.

6. GOD'S SAVING WORK: Personal and Cosmic

=========

'YOU WILL BE SAVED!'

Bhaskar Rao grew up in a high-class devout Hindu family in Andra Pradesh, India. He loved and admired his grandad, a holy man who knew the Hindu Scriptures off by heart, and who performed all the correct rituals.

To Bhaskar's horror, when his grandad fell ill, the old man had no peace. Despite all his religious observances, he died in terror of what would come next.

Bhaskar concluded that his religion offered no real answers. In despair, he resolved to take his own life. The very day he intended to commit suicide, 'by chance' he heard someone preaching the gospel. All he remembers are the words 'Believe on the Lord Jesus Christ and *you will be saved* and have eternal life'. He had never come across such certainty! He was converted, baptised, and went on to share the gospel with others.[1]

'ALL NATIONS WILL BE BLESSED!'

Vishal Mangalwadi was also born in India. As a young man, he also searched for spiritual reality. It troubled him that millions of Indians were permanently trapped in poverty and a fatalistic worldview, because of the Hindu caste system. He found, when he set out to read the holy books of his own nation that they were not even translated into the languages of the ordinary people. But the Bible was! He read it, and was amazed to find that the thread running throughout the Bible is God's desire to bless **all** nations.

Vishal decided to investigate whether or not the Bible had brought any blessing to **his** home country of India. He came to realise that many of the benefits enjoyed by modern Indians, such as their written languages, political democracy and educational system had been secured by Christian missionaries:

We were always told that India's freedom was a result of Mahatma Gandhi's struggle; it was a surprise to learn that, in reality, India's

---

1   Carswell, D, *Real Lives* (Paternoster, 2001).

freedom was a fruit of the Bible. Before the Bible, our people did not even have the modern notions of nation or freedom.[2]

Vishal converted to Christianity. He has devoted his life to bringing the blessings of the gospel to his own nation, **and** to researching the blessings brought to the whole world through the Bible.

CHRIST CAME TO DESTROY THE DEVIL'S WORK

In the Garden of Eden, Satan incited rebellion against God. It resulted in misery for our first parents, and all their descendants. The natural order was also impacted. Creation itself is 'groaning'.[3]

Even as God pronounced judgement on our first parents, He promised that Satan's efforts to hijack the good creation would be defeated. The woman's offspring ('seed') would 'crush the head of the serpent'.[4] This promise would

---

2   Mangalwadi, V, *The Book That Made Your World: How the Bible Created the Soul of Western Civilization* (Thomas Nelson, 2011), pp. 55-6.

3   Romans 8:22.

4   Genesis 3:15.

be fulfilled when the eternal Son of God became man, born of a woman:

The reason the Son of God appeared was to destroy the works of the devil. (1 John 3:8)

At the heart of God's loving salvation purpose is the salvation of individuals: people He has set His love upon, who are united with His Son, and brought into the 'body of Christ', the Christian church.[5]

The joy and love eternally existing between the persons of the Trinity overflows to embrace and include forgiven sinners. As rebellious sinners who have 'suppressed the truth' about God, we would naturally never willingly submit to Him. We are commanded to repent and believe in Christ, but we are dead in our sins. When we look back on our conversion, we realise that it was a gift of grace. In God's mercy He set His love upon us from eternity past. He chose us, and has justified us (counted us as righteous because of Christ's work). He will work in us to make us holy (ongoing sanctification). When we die, our souls will go immediately into God's presence. When Christ returns, our bodies will be raised and glorified,

---

5   Ephesians 4:15-16.

to serve and enjoy God in the new heavens and earth for ever.[6]

The fact that salvation is a gift of grace, means that we can pray for the most hostile people to be shown that grace. Probably the most unlikely convert in history was the apostle Paul. He was confronted with the risen Christ while on a mission to murder Christians. He came to know the joy of acceptance with God, and then devoted his life to preaching the good news to others.

Paul was confident that the Old Testament promises – that **all** nations would be blessed through the 'seed of Abraham' – would certainly be fulfilled. He taught that Christ's work of redemption achieved the unravelling of the curse in every respect.[7]

That does not mean that every single human being will be saved. But it does mean that although the whole created order has been affected by sin, it will be restored. God has great purposes for all of His creation. He does not give up on the work of His hands.

---

6   For more on this, you could read *A Student's Guide to Glorification* by Derek Thomas (Christian Focus Publications, 2021).

7   Colossians 1:20.

Your Christian faith is not just private! It's good news for all people and all creation.

When God has sent spiritual awakenings in the past, they have been accompanied with a host of social initiatives, as believers have sought to 'love thy neighbour'. As Christian missionaries have taken the good news of salvation to many different people groups, they have also taken blessings of education, healthcare, social reform and political freedoms.[8]

Christ defeated all evil when He rose from the dead and ascended to His Father's right hand. But we won't see the full outworking of this triumph until He returns. Then, all evil will be judged, and the earth itself will be renewed and restored.[9]

Think back to those two young men mentioned at the beginning of this chapter.

When Bhaskar Rao heard the good news of salvation offered to individual sinners, he turned to Christ, and found the joy and peace his religious observance had never achieved.

---

8   Soo James, S, *How Christianity Transformed the World* (Christian Focus, 2021).

9   2 Corinthians 5:10; Acts 3:21; Romans 8:21; 2 Peter 3:11-13.

When Vishal Mangalwadi discovered that Christ's triumph over evil had positively impacted so many aspects of life in his own nation, he was persuaded to become a Christian himself.

The Christian message of salvation is **both** transformative for individuals, **and** the means by which the whole world will ultimately be blessed. The biblical worldview assures us that God has good purposes for this world. He graciously continues to bless all people and restrain sin. When the principles of His moral law are followed, societies flourish. Human rebellion means that we won't see perfect justice until the return of Christ, but then all evil will be judged. The whole creation will be restored to what it was originally intended to be: a world of love, beauty, joy, fulfilment and praise to God. He will eternally be glorified in all and by all.

As the great hymn-writer Isaac Watts wrote:

He comes to make His blessings flow
Far as the curse is found.[10]

---

10   Watts, I, 'Joy to the World'.

Main point

Christ's saving work has personal, cosmic and eternal implications.

Questions for Reflection

- Why is the gospel good news for individuals?
- Why is the gospel good news for the whole world?

7. LOVE: Created to Relate and to Care

Eight-year-old Rachel Beckwith assumed that everyone has access to clean water. After all, when she turned a tap, water always flowed out! But one Sunday morning at church she learned that millions of children in the world have no access to safe water. She asked her mother if, instead of having a ninth birthday party, she could send a donation to *Charity: water*. The friends who would have come to her party could be invited to give donations as well. A gift of $220 was duly sent off.

Just five weeks later, tragically, Rachel was fatally injured in a road accident. After her death, the story of her kindness went viral, and $1.2 million was raised for *Charity: water* in her honour.[1]

---

1   Charity: water, 'Rachel's Legacy', https://medium.com/@charitywater/rachels-legacy-6ba639dbbd31, (accessed 11 August 2021).

IT'S NOT JUST 'ALL ABOUT ME'!

When I trained as a teacher, we were often told that 'self-actualisation' was the goal for every child. That sort of thinking fuels the idea that 'life is all about me'. Individual liberation and fulfilment are viewed as all-important. Independence is the goal. Don't be tied down by having others depend on you! And don't depend on others!

This worldview runs contrary to our creation design. When we are born, we are totally dependent on our parents for care, not just for weeks or months, but for our early years. As we grow in maturity and strength, we can help and care for others. Then, when we are old, we're likely once again to depend on others for care.

We are not strong and independent all our lives! That should make us both humble and grateful. We should be thankful for those who have cared for us (beginning with our parents or other carers). In turn, we are also 'wired up' to find joy and satisfaction in caring for others.

For all eternity, there was love between God the Father, Son and Holy Spirit. Relationship is at the heart of who God is. That great eternal fountain of love flowed out as God created this world. People created in His image were designed to enjoy His love. As the great medieval thinker Thomas Aquinas taught: 'Sheer joy is God's, and that demands companionship.'

All human beings are created in the image of God, for relationship with God and with others. He gives us the capacity to love and to care. We are commanded to:

> *Love the Lord your God with all your heart and with all your soul and with all your mind and with all your strength, and love your neighbour as yourself. (Mark 12:30-31)*

God designed that we should live in families and communities, as the context in which we give and receive love and care. In every family and community there are people with a whole range of needs. God has given us all a conscience, and an instinct that it is right to help the needy.

> *The righteous care about justice for the poor; but the wicked have no such concern. (Prov. 29:7)*

He who gives to the poor will lack nothing,
but he who closes his eyes to them receives
many curses. (Prov. 28:27)

God Himself has deep concern for the needy.[2]
He will hold us all accountable for how we treat
others.

Those who live only for themselves are
never truly fulfilled and joyful.[3] We are
designed to find joy in helping others. When
we see non-Christian people demonstrating
care and compassion, we should be grateful.
Tell them you're thankful! But give thanks to
God for them too! Their love and compassion
demonstrate that they are not just a random
collection of atoms. They have been created by
a loving God.

We are all called to love our neighbour.
That means seeking to do good to others, and
providing for the needs of those who suffer.[4]
It also means challenging the policies that

---

2   Psalm 12:5; 72:2,4.

3   Some secular research projects have supported
    this contention, for example: https://www.
    psychologytoday.com/us/blog/fulfillment-any-
    age/202108/how-caring-about-others-benefits-your-
    own-mental-health (accessed 9 February, 2022).

4   James 2:14-16, 17, 26.

damage our neighbour's well-being, and even destroy innocent life. We don't have to wait until everyone is converted before we can speak out in society about the ethics of caring for others. When we speak out in defence of protecting life, we can trust and pray that this will resonate with others made in the image of God. We should be informed and willing to engage with issues such as abortion, or the use of human embryos for research, or assisted suicide and euthanasia, or human trafficking, and many other ways in which human beings are being harmed.

In loving God, and loving and caring for others, we fulfil our creation design. Little Rachel Beckwith found joy in helping others. That was a small, but very beautiful reflection of the love of her Creator.

Main point

We are all called to love our neighbour.

Questions for Reflection

- Consider people who have shown you love and care. How could you cultivate a thankful spirit and show them gratitude?

- Who could you show care and concern for? What practical ways could you demonstrate that care?

8. SECURITY: Created to Belong

It was 1969. A group of women in New York City had gathered for a 'consciousness-raising' session. They began with a back-and-forth recitation, chanting:

'Why are we here today?'
 'To make Revolution!'
'And how do we make Revolution?'
 'By destroying the American family!'
'How do we do that?'
 'By destroying monogamy!'[1]

Such meetings, held across America and beyond, were the brainchild of **Kate Millett (1934-2017)**, a pioneer of radical feminism. She argued that women through the ages

---

1   https://www.frontpagemag.com/fpm/240037/
    marxist-feminisms-ruined-lives-mallory-millett
    (accessed 13 September, 2018). Monogamy is the
    belief that a person should just marry one person,
    not more than one.

had been oppressed by **patriarchy** (a word that gets thrown around a lot today! It comes from the Greek words *pater* for father, and *arche* for rule). Kate had suffered at the hands of an abusive father. She believed that the heterosexual married family was the main cause of female suffering. She initiated women's studies courses, and consciousness-raising groups, where women were taught that the family creates injustice. If family interfered with a woman's freedom, the woman should leave.

This played into a wider movement during the twentieth century which challenged 'systemic heteronormativity'.[2] Structures such as the man-woman married family, it was argued, 'privilege' straight people. They must be overthrown in order to achieve equality of dignity for LGBTQ+ people. Hence the slogans:

Smash the family!
Smash heteronormativity!
Love wins!
Families come in all shapes and sizes!
Gender is just a social construct!

---

2   Heteronormativity is the idea that sexual relations between a man and a woman are natural or normal.

This thinking is still promoted. In 2020, one radical feminist author argued that the family should be abolished, because it 'genders' us. Babies should be everyone's responsibility, belonging to nobody in particular.[3]

By the twentieth century the idea had gained ground that we are not accountable to anyone other than ourselves. There is no God, so there won't be a judgement. We can live free of the constraints of traditional morality or religious codes. But the dream of unlimited personal freedom always turns into nightmare. When moral norms break down, the powerful exploit the weak. Sexual 'liberation' has resulted in historically unprecedented global rates of pornography, which means sex trafficking, twisted expectations of sexual relationships, and an ocean of suffering for countless victims.

As intellectuals in university departments abandoned belief in a Creator God, they also insisted that there are no 'natural' structures for family and community. We can make our own

---

3   Lewis, S, 'The coronavirus crisis shows it's time to abolish the family', *Open Democracy*, 24 March 2020, https://www.opendemocracy.net/en/oureconomy/ coronavirus-crisis-shows-its-time-to-abolish-family/ (accessed 9 September, 2020); *Full Surrogacy Now: Feminism Against Family* (Verso, 2019), pp. 167-8.

rules. We're told that everyone has the right to 'discover' their own gender identity.[4] Everyone should have the right to have children, on their own if they want, by means of artificial reproductive technologies. It's regarded as unfair to 'privilege' man-woman marriage. You may be condemned as bigoted if you question the assertion that two men can make a baby.

CREATED TO BELONG

The truth, however, is found in both nature and Scripture. Biology points to the complementarity of sexes. It demonstrates the wondrous capacity of the male-female union to create new life.

The Bible teaches that marriage and parenthood are God's gift for **all** societies at **all** times. They formed part of the creation mandate (or command).[5] Jesus and Paul affirmed that Genesis 2 is foundational for understanding marriage.[6] The seventh command says that

---

4   For more on this, you could read my book *Gender Ideology: What Do Christians Need to Know?* (Christian Focus Publications, 2019).

5   Genesis 1:28; 2:20-25.

6   Matthew 19:5; 1 Corinthians 6:16; Ephesians 5:31.

marriage partners must be faithful to each other.[7]

Marriage provides children with ongoing care from the two people whose love gave them life. It links previous generations with future generations, providing each child with a genealogy, the knowledge of where they've come from. It's the foundational building block of all societies.[8]

God designed marriage to be a signpost to a greater eternal reality, the love of Christ for His Church.[9] But marriage is a temporary signpost; it's only for this life. We do not need to be married to be fulfilled as human beings. Jesus and Paul were both single. Equally, we should not demean family life.

The fifth commandment is for children to honour their parents. The book of Proverbs is filled with exhortations for sons and daughters to respect their mothers and fathers.[10] Jesus Christ obeyed His earthly parents.[11]

---

7 Exodus 20: 12,14.

8 https://www.christian.org.uk/wp-content/uploads/biblical-basis-of-marriage.pdf (Last accessed March 2022.)

9 Ephesians 5:22-33.

10 Eg. Proverbs 1:8; 3:1-2; 6:20; 13:1; 20:20.

11 Luke 2:51.

CHURCH AS FAMILY

It is true that sin brought conflict into family relationships.[12] Paul warned fathers not to be unreasonable with their children. He urged husbands not to be harsh with their wives.[13] And, sadly, children are sometimes left without one or both of their parents, by death, family breakdown or other factors.

The gospel can bring powerful comfort to those who have been robbed of the security of knowing who their natural parents are, and cheated of the care they should have been given. As a donor-conceived child, Louise Jamieson struggled for many years with a deep sense of loss. She didn't know who her own father was, but testifies:

Without faith in a God who is Father, I would still be floundering.[14]

The Bible commands that orphans should be cared for. Adoption can be a wonderful provision for such children (and it reflects the

---

12 Genesis 3:12,16.

13 Ephesians 6:4; 1 Peter 3:7.

14 Jamieson, L, 'The DI Journey: Pain, Loss and Discovery', in McWhinnie, A, ed, *Who Am I? Experiences of Donor Conception* (Idreos Education Trust, 2006), p. 35.

beauty of God's adoption of His people as His own children). Many Christians open their homes and offer hospitality to those who don't have loving family of their own.

Stuart grew up in an unhappy home, without his own dad. As a teenager, when his mother's new partner moved in, Stuart was thrown out. Although he'd had to leave school early, he worked hard to get a place at university to study engineering. There, he was invited to a little local church by a classmate. Stuart had never heard the good news of forgiveness. He became a Christian and found acceptance with God.

Although Stuart had no home of his own to return to during the holidays, he found a welcome in Christian homes. One particular family invited him for lunch every Sunday. The first time the mother of the family gave him a hug, he was overwhelmed. He'd never received that basic familial affection.

Stuart Burgess went on to become a world leader in engineering design. He has won many global awards and has also written books showing that design in nature points to the Creator God. He and his wife have five children. He's been able to provide them with the security and care that he sadly never received from his own dad.[15]

WHAT ABOUT KATE?

At the beginning of this chapter, we noted that Kate Millett encouraged countless women to leave their families. Kate's older sister, Mallory, recalls that over the years she has heard over and over again:

> *Your sister's books destroyed **my** sister's life! ... [My sister] was happily married with four kids, and after she read those books, [she] walked out on a bewildered man and didn't look back. The man fell into despairing rack and ruin. The children were stunted, set off their tracks, deeply harmed ...[16]*

Another broken family. A further weakening of those social bonds which make for strong, stable and happy communities.

---

15 'Real Lives: Interview with Stuart Burgess and Roger Carswell', Above Bar Baptist Church, 2015, https://www.youtube.com/watch?v=g7lTbgVNhMM (accessed 6 August, 2021).

16 https://www.frontpagemag.com/fpm/240037/marxist-feminisms-ruined-lives-mallory-millett (accessed 13 September, 2018).

Sin has spoiled family life. But the answer is not to get rid of the natural family! God created humans as male or female. Man-woman marriage is **not** just a social construct. It's His good design. It's good for society, and it's good for children.

Statistically, the safest place for a child to be, is with their own biological married parents. Broken relationships and fractured families result in a 'wail of anguish, which crescendos to the furthest reaches of our society'.[17] Some state workers may work hard to care for children in troubled circumstances, but they are not a substitute for the design God established at creation.

Today, sadly, many have experienced broken bonds. They long for fidelity and security. But we have a faithful God who keeps His promises. He has created us in His image, and His moral law works for human flourishing, not against it. And, as Stuart Burgess discovered, the powerful bonds of genuine Christian community can provide acceptance, commitment and grace.

---

17 James, O, *Britain on the Couch* (Century, 1997), p. 128.

Main point

God designed the family to mirror the faithfulness and love that He Himself shows to His people.

Questions for Reflection

- In what ways do you see God's design for the family being challenged today?
- In what ways has God designed marriage to reflect His own faithful character and also provide care between the generations?

9. TRUTH: Created to Learn

'There is no such thing as a neutral or objective claim' …The professor was explaining to our class that there is no such thing as capital-T Truth. **There is no right and wrong, no good and evil,** *he taught. We must always remember that we are subjective beings, and as such all our values are subjective.*[1]

Today at college or university, you're likely to be told at some point that the only **really** wrong thing is to believe in absolute truth and absolute morality. It's harmful to be restricted by religious laws or social conventions.

---

1   Shapiro, B, *Brainwashed: How Universities Indoctrinate America's Youth* (Thomas Nelson, 2010), p.1, emphasis mine.

In 2007, fourteen-year-old Yeonmi Park crossed a frozen river and three mountains in a desperate attempt to escape from North Korea. After suffering dreadful abuse in China, she made it safely to South Korea. In 2014, she secured a place at Columbia University, New York. Having experienced life in what is probably the least-free dictatorship on earth, she was eager to study in America, and looked forward to enjoying the freedom of thought she had been cruelly denied in her homeland.

Yeonmi had escaped the thought-police of North Korea. She assumed that now, at last, she'd be studying in a context of intellectual freedom. In reality, she had to censor all she said in New York as well! Her professors insisted that all of history and all of culture **had** to be seen through the lens of 'patriarchal, racist, heterosexist oppression'. Absolute personal freedom and absolute equality were viewed as all-important. Belief in absolute truth and morality was regarded as dangerous and wrong. Dissent from this prevailing worldview was not allowed.[2]

---

2 'The End of Universities?', The Jordan B. Peterson Podcast, S4: E:39, Aug 2, 2021, https://www. youtube.com/watch?v=dncyXvPR8uU, (accessed 10 August, 2021).

A worldview which demands unlimited individual freedom, not only rejects the idea of absolute truth and morality, but no longer tolerates any expression of belief in those ideas. It's a worldview that is deeply hostile to biblical Christianity.

This worldview makes sense when you throw out the idea of a God who defines truth and morality. If there's no transcendent authority, who can judge between competing claims? We can each make our own 'truth' and decide for ourselves what's right. No one is allowed to question **our** perception of reality (which may be based on our subjective experience). It's considered wrong and judgemental to fail to affirm other people's decisions. It's often taken to mean that we do not respect them as human beings.

'TRUTH CLAIMS ARE POWER GRABS!'

Many students are told that claims to absolute truth and universal explanations ('meta-narratives'), are simply power-grabs, used by privileged people in order to justify their own privilege. But when you deny the existence of objective universal truth it becomes impossible to have reasoned debate. The loudest voices win.

I remember how shocked I was the first time I was told that logic is a 'male' construct. Nothing could be more demeaning to women! Radical feminist, Audre Lorde, for example, believed that logic, reason, evidence and science are 'the master's tools'. That is, they are the methods used by 'racist, patriarchal' academics. Instead, one should rely on the lived experience of oppressed people.[3] Of course, it's important to listen to people's experiences, whoever they are. But we need to use reason and logic to assess their claims.

THERE IS UNIVERSAL TRUTH

The biblical worldview insists that the Creator God is a God of reason and truth. His creation reveals His power, glory and infinite wisdom. The extraordinary complexity of the design of every part of our universe reveals rational design. Logic, mathematics and musical principles are not invented by humans. They

---

3   Lorde, A, 'The Master's Tools Will Never Dismantle the Master's House', 1984, *Sister Outsider: Essays and Speeches*, ed. Berkeley, CA (Crossing Press, 2007), https://collectiveliberation.org/wp-content/uploads/2013/01/Lorde_The_Masters_Tools.pdf (accessed 6 August, 2020).

are hardwired into the way things are. They are there to be discovered.[4]

Humans created in God's image have the capacity to investigate and reason. God has endowed every person with the capacity to know, enjoy and serve Him. We know God through His Word, so everyone should be able to read the Bible, and have access to the Bible in their own language. Historically, Christians have been at the forefront of literacy provision worldwide.[5]

Christians have been at the forefront of pioneering educational provision worldwide as well, insisting that girls as well as boys should be educated.[6] That's because they know that God has endowed everyone with the capacity to reason, so that capacity should be developed. Every child should be educated, and each child's unique gifts and capacities should be nurtured and developed. The Christian hymn-

---

4   McDermott, G R, *Everyday Glory: The Revelation of God in all of Reality* (Baker Academic, 2018), pp. 45-84.

5   http://www.affinity.org.uk/downloads/The%20 Bulletin/issue-47/1)-educational-provision---final. pdf (Last accessed March 2022.)

6   James, S, *How Christianity Transformed the World*, chapter 8.

writer **Isaac Watts (1674-1748)**[7] was also a great educationalist. His best-selling book, *The Improvement of the Mind*, argued that we should go on learning all through our lives, developing the mind that God has given us.

THE UNIVERSE IS GOD'S BOOK

The heavens declare the glory of God, the skies proclaim the work of his hands. (Ps. 19:1)

The first universities throughout Europe, and then in America, were all Christian foundations. This, of course, is not just something for the West. The works of the Lord, and knowledge of those works, are universally available. We have all been created with the capacity to reason, explore and discover. To fully honour our Creator, we must study and appreciate His handiwork.

Sociologist Rodney Stark has argued convincingly that Christian theology was essential for the rise of science.[8] Christians such as Kepler, Newton, and Faraday believed

---

7   He wrote hymns such as 'Joy to the World', 'When I Survey the Wondrous Cross', 'Alas and Did my Saviour Bleed', and 'Jesus Shall Reign Where'er the Sun'.

8   Stark, R, *For the Glory of God*, p. 123; pp. 121-99.

that the whole universe is like a book written by God, waiting to be read and understood by people made in His image. It can only be understood because the faithful God ensures that it functions according to reliable principles. The entire universe is held together by Christ.[9]

The great German astronomer **Johannes Kepler (1571-1630)** believed that God created us in His image so that we could share His thoughts after Him.[10] God founded the universe in an ordered way: we are capable of exploring and studying it.

Isaac Newton (1642-1727) pioneered understanding of light, and the laws of motion and gravity. His development of the calculus is the foundation of modern physics. For Newton, the beautiful order and lawfulness of the universe could not be explained in impersonal or mechanical terms. God is the Maker of all things visible and invisible.[11]

Despite his towering genius, Newton remained humble. He knew that the infinite God

---

9   Colossians 1:17; Hebrews 1:3; Acts 17:28.

10   Kepler, J, quoted in Ryken, P G, *Christian Worldview: A Student's Guide* (Crossway, 2013), p. 59.

11   Stark, R, *For the Glory of God*, pp. 167-72.

has created an infinitely wonderful universe. There will always be more to discover.

> *I do not know what I may appear to the world, but to myself I seem to have been only like a boy playing on the sea-shore, and diverting myself finding now and again a smoother pebble or a prettier shell than ordinary, while the great ocean of truth lay all unknown before me.*[12]

Michael Faraday (1791-1867) was brought up in poverty, spent much of his childhood on the streets, and had little schooling. But when he read Isaac Watts' *The Improvement of the Mind,* he was so inspired that he determined to educate himself. After attending public lectures given by the famous Sir Humphrey Davy, he plucked up courage to apply to become Davy's assistant. He steadily worked his way up to become the leading scientist of his day. Even after he was working at the Royal Institution, he went without dinner every other day in order to pay for his young sister's schooling.[13]

---

12 Newton, I, quoted in Bragg, M, *12 Books that Changed the World*, p. 31.

13 Masters, P, 'Michael Faraday: Scientist and Christian', *Evangelical Times*, (December 2003), https://www. evangelical-times.org/articles/historical/michael-

TRUTH: Created to Learn

The discovery of how to harness the power of electricity was just one of his achievements. His public lectures were packed out, and sometimes attended by celebrities such as Charles Dickens, Charles Darwin and Prince Albert. As a devout Christian, who preached regularly in his chapel, Faraday regarded his scientific research as 'reading the book of nature, written by the finger of God'.[14]

Science is a universal discipline. It can be engaged in by people whatever their group identity. Logic, science, mathematics and engineering are not 'tools' of oppression (although in a sinful world they can be abused). They can be applied to liberate people from poverty and hunger, protect people from sickness and natural disaster, and provide numerous benefits.

At the beginning of this chapter, we encountered Professor Joshua Muldaven of UCLA telling his class that there is no such thing as good and evil, and that all values are subjective. Freshman Ben Shapiro was in that class. His reaction?

---

faraday-scientist-and-christian/ (accessed 11 August, 2021).

14 James Hamilton, quoted in Bragg, M, *12 Books that Changed the World*, p. 221.

It's a load of bunk. Of course evil exists. Anyone who believes there is an excuse for rape is evil. Anyone who believes in killing disabled children is evil. Anyone who flies planes into buildings with the intent of killing civilians is evil.[15]

God is not silent. He has revealed Himself in Creation and in His Word. Morality, truth and justice are grounded in the nature of God.[16] We can be confident that there is such a thing as universal truth.

Main point
Morality, truth and justice are grounded in the nature of God.

Questions for Reflection
- Why do you think Christians have been at the forefront of educational provision worldwide?
- Some claim that 'Christianity is the enemy of science'. How would you respond?

---

15 Shapiro, B, *Brainwashed: How Universities Indoctrinate America's Youth*, p.1.

16 Jeremiah 9:24.

10. FULFILMENT: Created to Create

Henry IV acceded to the throne of France in 1589. Many years of civil war had left the nation in dire poverty. Henry vowed to ensure that every family would be able to afford a chicken in the pot every Sunday. Helped by his chief advisor, the Duke of Sully, a remarkable transformation took place.

Throughout his long life Sully was driven to innovate, to create and to problem-solve. He was a brilliant financier, engineer, agriculturalist, military advisor and politician. He organised a programme of works to build the infrastructure of France (bridges, roads, hospitals, schools, fortifications, and a canal system to link up the major rivers). To liberate commerce, he abolished road tolls, and created a national postal service. He probably organised the planting of more trees than anyone else in history. He promoted new agricultural methods, and oversaw draining and reclamation which doubled the area of productive farmland. Sully sponsored new industrial techniques and organised the rebuilding of Paris. Living conditions improved immeasurably. And more families enjoyed that chicken in the pot each Sunday!

THE BLESSINGS OF FREEDOM

During the Protestant Reformation, a large proportion of the French population had converted to the Reformed faith. Nicknamed the 'Huguenots', they lived out John Calvin's conviction that God should be glorified in **all** of life.[1] During the reign of Henry IV, peace and liberty of conscience enabled them to found schools and build churches. They became leaders in agriculture, trade, and the textile, paper, iron and printing industries. They were famous for their beautiful designs and craftsmanship. Many Huguenots, including the Duke of Sully, made an immense contribution to the well-being of France.

---

1   https://www.christian.org.uk/wp-content/uploads/huguenots.pdf (Last accessed March 2022.)

THE EVILS OF TYRANNY

Henry IV's grandson Louis XIV ended the toleration which had enabled people such as the Duke of Sully to prosper. Known as 'The Sun King', Louis XIV claimed *L'Etat – C'est Moi.*[2] Like tyrants everywhere, he claimed absolute power and crushed individual liberty. He persecuted the Huguenots to the point that he claimed that there weren't any left. In 1685, he revoked the Edict of Nantes (which had granted a measure of tolerance). Now, all Protestant worship was to be suppressed.

That was one of the worst decisions ever made by a ruler.

'This dreadful plot of the king has depopulated a quarter of France,' lamented one Frenchman. As hundreds of thousands of Huguenots fled, France suffered through the exodus of talented and industrious workers, including skilled silversmiths, weavers, linen-workers, lace-makers, and clockmakers. Surrounding countries were greatly enriched.

CREATED TO CREATE

God's common grace equips humans to work together in communities where we cooperate

2   'L'Etat, c'est moi' can be translated, 'The State – is ME!' The King was claiming absolute power.

to do what we could not do alone. He gives the capacity to create wealth by producing goods and services. We should be thankful to God for the abilities and skills of all the different people who serve our needs.

[Work] is a practical way of showing neighbour love. It makes cities thrive, keeps the streets clean, makes the soil productive, keeps dinner on the table and clothes clean, makes people attractive, heals through medicine, instructs people in schools, makes the economy work ... and connects people ... [3]

The creation command (or mandate)[4] was for our first parents, and those coming after them, to fill the earth and manage it for God. The fourth commandment refers back to creation, and so is for all people in all times.

Remember the Sabbath day to keep it holy. **Six days shall you labour** *... for in six days the Lord made the heavens and earth and everything in them. (Exod. 20:8-11)*

---

3   R. Paul Stevens, *The Abolition of the Laity: Vocation, Work and Ministry in a Biblical Perspective* (Paternoster, 1999), p.125.

4   Genesis 1:28.

God is the Lord of all creation. He allows human beings to function as 'his hands and arms' to carry on the creative process.[5] He gives us all different skills and abilities.[6] This is not just paid work, it includes home-making, child-care, economics, art, music, literature, science, cooking, agriculture, architecture and engineering.

We see works of art in every culture and civilisation. When someone creates something of beauty, it is not just for self-fulfilment. We find delight in giving pleasure to others and providing for their needs. That capacity did not evolve by chance. It is the gift of God.

We will give account to our Creator for the work that we do.[7] Work is a blessing, because it enables us to provide for ourselves, our families and the needy.[8]

The fourth commandment reminds us that we are also to rest. A day to stop work is a gift from our Creator. He modelled this pattern

5 John L. Mackay, *The Dignity of Work, The Christian Institute*, 2011, https://www.christian.org.uk/wp-content/uploads/dignityofwork.pdf, p. 13. (Last accessed March 2022.)

6 Exodus 35:30-3.

7 Romans 14:12; Colossians 3:23-4.

8 2 Thessalonians 3:7-10; Ephesians 4:28.

Himself in the creation week. On this special day, we can fulfil our creation purpose: to remember our Creator and worship Him.

God designs that we should learn from the wisdom of the past, building on the learning and achievements of those who have gone before. That is the importance of the task of education and the importance of history: respecting collective memory and accumulated wisdom.

WORK AND THE FALL

The entry of sin into the world has affected our work. It is often difficult, frustrating, and seemingly unrewarding.[9] We may see injustice and inequality at work, as well as in society.

Capitalism has been discredited because of human greed and selfishness. Because of human sin, we see financial scandal, ostentatious consumerism, waste, and despoiling of the environment. However, the answer isn't to reject wealth creation and private property! Those same evils flourish in socialist and communist systems (albeit among the ruling elite while the vast majority live in dire poverty). And when freedom to create

---

9   Genesis 3:17-19.

wealth is thrown out, every marker of human flourishing decreases.

By 1980 about 28 nations, representing more than 1.5 million people (more than one-third of the world's population) were governed by Marxist regimes.[10] All were characterised by loss of individual freedom, widespread poverty and suppression of religious practice.

The great socialist experiment in Venezuela has been a catastrophe. Latin America's once most prosperous state has been reduced to penury. Thriving private enterprises have been replaced with desperate bartering. By 2018 more than 2.3 million Venezuelans had attempted to escape.[11]

Over the past couple of centuries there has been a remarkable reduction in absolute global poverty.[12] That has not been caused by

10 Blanchard, J, *Does God Believe in Atheists?* p. 69.

11 Mitchell, J, 'Maduro's Madness: How Venezuela's Great Socialist Experiment has brought a Country to its Knees', *The Spectator*, (25 August 2018), https://www.spectator.co.uk/article/maduro-s-madness (accessed 30 July, 2020).

12 https://www.firstthings.com/web-exclusives/2013/11/whats-behind-the-stunning-decrease-in-global-poverty, (accessed 12 August, 2021); 'What Caused The Economic Boom of Wealth?' *Learn Liberty*, (29 April 2014), https://www.

massive redistribution of resources, or punitive payments of reparations, or foreign aid. It's been caused by innovation: people solving problems, creating businesses, providing others with employment, and supplying human needs. It's happened because in some nations there has been freedom to create wealth.[13]

Free societies ensure **equal opportunities.** All human beings made in God's image should have the opportunity to flourish. That's why universal education, including for women, is so important.

But because humans are individuals, we are all different. We vary in ability, competence, energy, motivation and integrity. To **enforce equal outcomes** demands state intervention in every aspect of life. It signals the end of a free society.

Free societies enable people to work with the assurance that their property will be protected, not wilfully requisitioned by the State. It's impossible for people to escape from

---

youtube.com/watch?v=a0nsKBx77EQ, (accessed 17 August, 2021).

13 Grudem, W, Asmus, B, *The Poverty of Nations: a Sustainable Solution* (Crossway, 2013), chapters 1-5.

poverty in nations where they cannot secure documented property ownership.[14]

God ultimately owns the whole earth, but property does not belong to the government or to society as a whole. The eighth commandment, 'You shall not steal', implies the legitimacy of owning private property.[15]

We are here on this earth to bring glory to our Creator. We will answer to Him for how we use the talents He has entrusted to us.[16] The *way* that we work (our character) is just as important as *what* we achieve. We are to work for God's glory and the good of our fellow human beings.

Just like those skilled and industrious Huguenots who brought such blessings to other countries, when thrown out by their own.

Main point

God's common grace equips humans to work together in communities where we cooperate to do what we could not do alone.

---

14   Ibid., p. 151.

15   Exodus 20:15.

16   1 Peter 4:10; Matthew 25:14-30.

Questions for Reflection

- In what ways is work a blessing?
- In what ways has work been impacted by sin?

Conclusion

Think back to journalist Douglas Murray. Travelling to countries where the Christian worldview had crumbled, he noted the lack of meaning and purpose among many young people. *'Is this all there is?'* they wonder, as they live from one social gathering to the next.

Such young people need to hear the good news of the gospel! They need to know that **the biblical worldview shows us that:**

- We have been created by the supremely great and glorious God to know and enjoy Him.
- We can find forgiveness and reconciliation with our Creator.
- We can then find meaning, purpose and joy as we love Him and serve others.

The biblical worldview provides:

- The only solid foundation for human dignity. *Every* person should be afforded equal dignity and value, because each one has been created in the image of God.

- The only solid foundation for real freedom. No government, academic institution, or employer has the authority to tell us what to think. We will each answer to God.

- The only solid foundation for morality. If we are not accountable to God and each make our own rules, the result is moral relativism. But the perfectly just and righteous God has given us all a conscience, an awareness of His moral law.

- The only sure way to human flourishing. Even in a sinful world, God provides blessing to all. Family, work and civil authorities have been impacted by sin, but they are God's provision for our good.

Today many people are hostile to the Christian faith, and in the face of this, many Christians are intimidated. But we have every reason to be confident. The gospel really is good news! And people around us need to hear it.

Appendix A: What Now?

- Begin each day with praise to God.
- Cultivate an attitude of gratitude towards others.
- Be aware that the worldview of many people around you may be fundamentally opposed to the biblical worldview. 'Test all things' – what does the Word of God say?
- We are told to 'be prepared to give an answer to everyone who asks you to give the reason for the hope that you have' (1 Pet. 3:15). That means reading, study and reflection. Use the 'further reading' at the end of this book, and other TRACK resources to help you do this.
- As we prepare to 'give an answer', we are told to 'do this with gentleness and respect' (1 Pet. 3:15). Pray for those who may oppose your biblical testimony. What they

say is wrong, but you are called to be kind, as you relate to them.

- At the root of today's unbiblical worldviews is the theory of evolution, the idea that there is no Creator God, and the assumption that we are not morally accountable to our Creator. Get informed about some of the ways that evolution is a 'theory in crisis' (some resources suggested in Appendix B).

Appendix B: Other Books and Resources

―――――

OVERVIEW OF HOW CHRISTIANITY HAS BROUGHT POSITIVE BENEFITS TO THE WORLD:
James, S, *How Christianity Transformed the World,* (Christian Focus, 2021)

This book will help you respond to the claims often made that Christianity has been a toxic and repressive influence in history.

EXPLANATION OF THE NEGATIVE IMPACT OF UNBIBLICAL WORLDVIEWS:
James, S, *The Lies We Are Told: The Truth We Must Hold,* (Christian Focus, 2022)

This book will help you respond to issues like critical theory, including critical race theory, as well as other challenges to the biblical worldview.

HOW TO RESPOND TO CURRENT CLAIMS ABOUT GENDER:

James, S, *Gender Ideology: What do Christians Need to Know?* (Christian Focus, 2019)

The idea that gender is fluid directly challenges the Christian worldview. This book provides a simple overview of gender ideology and how you can respond.

A COURSE TO HELP PUT THE BIBLICAL WORLDVIEW INTO PRACTICE:

livingchristianity.org.uk
livingchristianity.org.uk/youth

SOME RESOURCES ON BIBLICAL CREATION:

Biblical Creation Trust, https://www.biblicalcreationtrust.org/index.html

Burgess, S, *Genesis 1 & 2: A Scientist's Perspective*, https://www.podbean.com/media/share/pb-3dsxv-1047305?utm_campaign=w_share_ep&utm_medium=dlink&utm_source=w_share

Mohler, A, 'Why does the Universe look so Old?'
https://www.youtube.com/watch?v=AMNXC-_1R40

A MORE DETAILED BOOK ON CHRISTIAN WORLDVIEW:

Ryken, P G, *Christian Worldview: A Student's Guide* (Crossway, 2013)

BIBLICAL ANSWERS TO THE QUESTIONS MANY YOUNG PEOPLE ASK:

Robertson, D, *A.S.K. Real World Questions / Real Word Answers* (Christian Focus, 2019)

ONLINE BRIEFINGS ON SOME OF THE THEMES OF THIS BOOK:

Judge, M, *The Biblical Basis of Marriage,* https://www.christian.org.uk/wp-content/uploads/biblical-basis-of-marriage.pdf

Ling, J R, *When Does Human Life Begin?* https://www.christian.org.uk/wp-content/uploads/when-does-human-life-begin.pdf

Mackay, J L, *The Dignity of Work,* https://www.christian.org.uk/wp-content/uploads/dignityofwork.pdf

Mackay, J L, T*he Moral Law,* https://www.christian.org.uk/wp-content/uploads/the-moral-law.pdf

Needham, N R, *Common Grace*, https://www.christian.org.uk/wp-content/uploads/common-grace.pdf

Appendix C: The Ten Commandments and the Lord's Prayer

THE TEN COMMANDMENTS

1 You shall have no other gods before me.

2 You shall not make for yourself an image in the form of anything in heaven above or on the earth beneath or in the waters below. You shall not bow down to them or worship them.

3 You shall not misuse the name of the Lord your God, for the Lord will not hold anyone guiltless who misuses his name.

4 Remember the Sabbath day by keeping it holy. Six days you shall labor and do all your work, but the seventh day is a sabbath to the Lord your God. For in six days the Lord made the heavens and the earth, the sea, and all that is in them, but he rested on the seventh day. Therefore the Lord blessed the Sabbath day and made it holy.

5 Honor your father and your mother, so that you may live long in the land the Lord your God is giving you.

6 You shall not murder.

7 You shall not commit adultery.

8 You shall not steal.

9 You shall not give false testimony against your neighbor.

10 You shall not covet anything that belongs to your neighbor. (See Exod. 20:3-17)

JESUS' SUMMARY OF THE LAW

Love the Lord your God with all your heart and with all your soul and with all your mind. This is the first and greatest commandment. And the second is like it: 'Love your neighbor as yourself.' All the Law and the Prophets hang on these two commandments. (Matt. 22:37-40)

THE LORD'S PRAYER

Our Father in heaven,
hallowed be your name,
your kingdom come,
your will be done, on earth as it is in heaven.

Give us today our daily bread.
And forgive us our debts, as we also have
forgiven our debtors.
And lead us not into temptation, but deliver
us from the evil one. (Matt. 6:9-13)

Acknowledgments

Some of the material in this book has been given in talks given at Word Alive (an annual Bible teaching conference for students and others in the UK). Some has also appeared in other articles, books, and talks. I have tried to acknowledge this where appropriate. I am grateful to Rosanna Burton and John Perritt for all their help with this book.

It is a privilege to work as part of a team at The Christian Institute, UK (christian.org.uk). The views expressed in this book are my own, as are any and all mistakes made.

Sharon James
London, 2022

Reformed Youth Ministries (RYM) exists to serve the Church in reaching and equipping youth for Christ. Passing on the faith to the next generation has been RYM's mission since it began. In 1972, three youth workers who shared a passion for biblical teaching to high school students surveyed the landscape of youth ministry conferences. What they found was a primary emphasis on fun and games, not God's Word. They launched a conference that focused on the preaching and teaching of God's Word – RYM. Over the last five decades RYM has grown from a single summer conference into three areas of ministry: conferences, training, and resources.

- **Conferences:** RYM hosts multiple summer conferences for local church groups in a variety of locations across the United States. Conferences are for either middle school or high school students and their leaders.
- **Training:** RYM launched an annual Youth Leader Training (YLT) event in 2008. YLT is

for anyone serving with youth in the local church. YLT has grown steadily through the years and is now offered in multiple locations. RYM also offers a Church Internship Program in partnering local churches, youth leader coaching and youth ministry consulting services.

- **Resources:** RYM offers a growing array of resources for leaders, parents, and students. Several BIble studies are available as free downloads (new titles regularly added). RYM hosts multiple podcasts available on numerous platforms: The Local Youth Worker, Parenting Today, and The RYM Student Podcast. To access free downloads, for podcast information, and access to many additional ministry tools visit us on the web – rym.org.

RYM is a 501(c)(3) non-profit organization. Our mission is made possible through the generous support of individuals, churches, foundations and businesses that share our mission to serve the Church in reaching and equipping youth for Christ. If you would like to partner with RYM in reaching and equipping the next generation for Christ please visit rym.org/donate.

Christian Focus Publications

Our mission statement —

STAYING FAITHFUL

In dependence upon God we seek to impact the world
through literature faithful to His infallible Word, the Bible.
Our aim is to ensure that the Lord Jesus Christ is presented as
the only hope to obtain forgiveness of sin, live a useful life and
look forward to heaven with Him.

Our books are published in four imprints:

CHRISTIAN FOCUS

Popular works including biographies, commentaries, basic doctrine and Christian living.

CHRISTIAN HERITAGE

Books representing some of the best material from the rich heritage of the church.

MENTOR

Books written at a level suitable for Bible College and seminary students, pastors, and other serious readers. The imprint includes commentaries, doctrinal studies, examination of current issues and church history.

CF4•K

Children's books for quality Bible teaching and for all age groups: Sunday school curriculum, puzzle and activity books; personal and family devotional titles, biographies and inspirational stories — because you are never too young to know Jesus!

Christian Focus Publications Ltd,
Geanies House, Fearn, Ross-shire,
IV20 1TW, Scotland, United Kingdom.
www.christianfocus.com
blog.christianfocus.com